In honor of
two very special children

Lawrence & Gabriella Rivka

from their loving parents
Alan & Adele

KIND LITTLE RIVKA

FIRST EDITION
First Impression — November 1991

Published by HaChai Publishing

ISBN 0—922613—44-3 (Casebound Edition)
ISBN 0—922613—45-1 (Softcover Edition)

Distributed by HaChai Publishing
705 Foster Avenue
Brooklyn, N.Y. 11230
(718) 692-3900

Printed in Hong Kong

Kind
Little Rivka

By Dina Rosenfeld

Drawings by
Ilene Winn-Lederer

Hachai
PUBLISHING

A Note to Parents and Teachers

Kind Little Rivka is based on the Biblical account in the Book of Genesis of the early life of Rivka (Rebecca). Details taken from the Midrash provide additional background to this well-known story. We have included the following summary so you can better convey this famous tale to your child.

When Yitzchak (Isaac) was 40 years old and of marriageable age, his father Avraham (Abraham) was 140 years old and too weak to travel. Avraham was firm in his refusal to allow Yitzchak to marry one of the girls from the local Canaanite tribes. The entire destiny of the Jewish people relied on a union between Yitzchak and a woman from Avraham's family who possessed the proper spiritual qualities to establish a holy nation. Therefore, Avraham sent Eliezer, his trusted servant, to seek a wife for Yitzchak across the desert, where Avraham's brother, Nachor, lived. According to the Midrash, the 17-day trip from the land of Canaan to Aram Naharayim was miraculously completed by Eliezer just three hours after leaving his master's home.

Arriving at the well of Aram Naharayim, Eliezer devised a test to help him find a suitable wife for Yitzchak, and prayed to the A-mighty that it succeed. Since Avraham was renowned for his outstanding and unusual kindness to strangers, Eliezer wished to find that same quality of kindness in the prospective bride. The servant decided to ask each girl at the well for a drink of water. To pass the test, the right girl would have to provide him with a drink and offer to draw water for his camels.

Just then, Eliezer saw Rivka approaching the well. When he asked for a drink, she gave it to him graciously and immediately offered to water his camels. Not only did the three-year-old girl give each camel water to drink, but she exerted herself to provide enough water to fully satisfy the thirst of those huge animals. Only after she passed this test did Eliezer discover that Rivka was indeed from Avraham's family. She was the granddaughter of Avraham's brother, Nachor, making her eligible to marry Yitzchak.*

We hope your child will identify with the story of Rivka's generosity and strive to emulate her kind behavior toward others.

D. Rosenfeld

*According to other opinions, Rivka was 14 years old or in her thirties at the time of her marriage to Yitzchak.

Long, long ago, on one side of the desert, there lived a little girl named Rivka.

One day, when Rivka was three years old, she decided to go down to the well and bring back water for her family. She found an empty pitcher, lifted it high on her shoulder, and went on her way.

That very same day, on the other side
of the desert, a man named Eliezer
began walking with ten camels following
behind him. The camels were loaded
with bags full of presents; shiny golden
bracelets and rings, beautiful new
dresses, and just about anything
else a little girl could want.

Eliezer was looking for a kind and special girl to be a wife for Yitzchak, the son of Avraham. "When I find the right girl," thought Eliezer, "she will get all of these wonderful presents."

Eliezer and the camels walked across the dry, empty desert, where no rains fall, no trees grow, and no cool winds blow.

It was hot, hot, hot in the desert.

Before long, Eliezer came to a well of water. He saw so many girls taking water from the well.

Some were tall, and some were short. There were girls with long, brown hair, and girls with big, dark eyes. "Which one will be the right wife for Yitzchak?" he wondered.

Then Eliezer had an idea. "I will ask each girl for a drink of water. The one who is kind enough to give water to me and to my camels will be the right wife for Yitzchak." Suddenly, Eliezer saw Rivka coming to the well with her pitcher on her shoulder.

On her way, she met a little boy. He was sitting on the ground with his head on his knees, crying softly to himself. "What is the matter?" asked little Rivka.

"Oh," sobbed the boy, "I hurt my foot on a sharp stone and I can't walk."

"I will help you!" said Rivka.

The little girl set down her pitcher and took off her scarf. As Eliezer watched, she wrapped it carefully around the boy's foot like a soft bandage.

The boy stood up and wiped his tears. "How kind you are, Rivka!" he said happily. "Now I can walk again!"

Rivka put her pitcher back on her shoulder and continued on her way. She walked along until she met a woman. The woman was wandering from one side of the road to the other. She seemed to be lost.

"What is the matter?" asked little Rivka. "I don't see very well," answered the woman, "and I can't find my way home." "I will help you," said Rivka.

As Eliezer watched, the little girl took the woman's hand and walked by her side until they reached the right house.

"Thank you, kind little Rivka," said the woman gratefully. "It's good to be back home." Rivka turned and hurried on her way.

When at last she reached the well, Rivka was tired. She sat down to rest on a smooth stone near the water.

Just then, an old man with white hair came over to the well. As Eliezer watched, the little girl jumped up and gave her seat to the old man.

"How kind you are, little Rivka," he said.
"It feels so good to rest my weary legs."

Finally, little Rivka bent down to fill her pitcher. How surprised she was when the water in the well came up to meet her!

Eliezer watched as the little girl put the heavy pitcher back on her shoulder. With slow steps, she turned to go home.

"Hmm," he thought. "This girl was kind to the little boy, she helped the woman find her way, and she gave her seat to the tired old man. But will she give me a drink of water? Will she want to be kind to my thirsty camels? If she gives water to me and to my camels, then I'll know she is the girl I've been looking for."

Eliezer ran over to Rivka and asked, "Please, may I have a little sip of water from your pitcher?"

When Rivka saw how hot and thirsty Eliezer looked, she held out her heavy pitcher and answered . . .

"Of course you may drink!"

All at once the little girl noticed the ten camels standing behind Eliezer. They had walked across the desert without a drink. Their throats were dry and scratchy. Their fur was hot and full of sand. They looked at the water with big, sad eyes. "Poor camels," thought Rivka.

When Eliezer had finished drinking, she said, "Now, I will also give water to your camels!"

And so she did.

Back and forth, back and forth went Rivka, filling and

spilling, pulling and pouring. She did not stop until all the thirsty camels had had enough to drink.

"She is so kind," thought Eliezer.
"Now I know I have found the
right girl for Yitzchak!"

Eliezer gave Rivka two shiny golden bracelets, a beautiful ring, and many other presents.

Best of all, kind little Rivka married Yitzchak and became one of the mothers of the Jewish people!

For a little girl named Alta Mina
צ"ה
who loved true stories.
D.R.

To Jeffrey, Joshua & Ira
with love
for the dreams we share.
I.W.L.